YOUNEEK STUDIOS

WINDMAKER™

THE HISTORY OF ATALA

THE ART OF THE BOOK SERIES

ISBN 9780996607063
Published by YouNeek Studios, Inc.

5401 McGrath Blvd. #813 North Bethesda MD 20852.

For All Inquiries Contact: info@youneekstudios.com

Creator, Writer
ROYE OKUPE

Illustrator
GODWIN AKPAN

Logo Design
PAUL LOUISE-JULIE

Additional Artwork
CHIMA KALU, RAPHAEL KAZEEM &
MOHAMMED AGBADI

Ming Concept Art
CHYI MING LEE, LESLIE NG KAZUKI, AARON LIN
WILLY WONG & KAIJU DEN LLP, SINGAPORE

Contents

Introduction

Dear reader,

The tome before you is a collection of the history of our great nation, Atala. As I sit here in Awori, one of the most beautiful places in the entire Oyo Kingdom, I ponder the journey ahead to reunite with my King, Bass Kazaar, who recently embarked on a journey of his own to Azzaz to visit Queen Malika. My mind is filled with thoughts on how far we have come as a nation. From the arrival of Atala, **The First Father** himself, along with his two children, Oris and Useh, to the grueling wars with the Ming Dynasty, our history is filled with humble beginnings, tempestuous streaks and astonishing triumphs.

I have taken it upon myself as one closest to our king to document these events from our rich history. Until now, I have seen no such compilation. It would be a shame for such knowledge and legacy to be lost in the embers of history. If you are wondering why a soldier is so concerned about history, well, it is because I was fortunate enough to visit the great Sankore Madrasah, in the Malian Empire, where I absorbed vast knowledge on linguistics, learning five different languages. I am simply a student trying to practice what I was taught.

Whoever, wherever and whenever you are reading this, I hope you can appreciate the rich history and culture of our great nation. And I hope you do the needful thing and spread the word of this great African kingdom. For one of the greatest sins I can imagine would be to bury or destroy such a delicate history. My wish is that centuries from now, future generations will look back on this with joy and pride about their heritage.

BENGU, TRUSTED ADVISOR TO THE KING

"A day will come when darkness will
return. From the depths he will rise
and we mortals will be the cause
of his return. War, oppression,
genocide, everything we have
done to express our hatred for one
another will empower him. But fear
not, for light will return as well. And
with light will come triumph. For
light travels fastest in darkness."

Wondu The Wise

1

THE DIVINE ONES

The Divine Ones

The all-powerful **Divine Ones**. Our deities. Said to have migrated from what is now the **Oyo Kingdom**, the Divine Ones comprise of Atala, along with his two sons **Oris** and **Useh**. A family of dragon riders as they were called back then, The Divine Ones were the most powerful beings of their era. But like most all-powerful families of gods, this power would cause dissent amongst their ranks. And this dissent came in form of what we Atalians call: the rage of Useh.

You see, back then as it is now, it was very common for offspring to worship their fathers. Seeking attention and acceptance. Year after year both sons, Oris and Useh, made sacrifices to please their father, Atala. However, Useh, ever the eager one, took many shortcuts in his ways. This displeased Atala who began to favor the more forbearing and wise Oris. Years passed and Oris became the clear favorite of the two, further driving Useh towards rage, jealousy and bitterness. And then came the tipping point. For his continued excellence, Oris was granted **Dragon's Destiny**, Atala's most prized possession and perhaps the most powerful weapon ever created.

Following this event, Useh went mad with rage. So much so that he manifested it as raw energy with the help of dark magic. Next, Useh used this new power to craft his own blade. A blade he called Dragon's Doom. Its power rivaled Dragon's Destiny. But Useh did not stop there. With **Dragon's Doom**, he set his sights on his own father. Atala was so weakened in his heart by his own son's betrayal, that he refused to fight him. Useh killed Atala without hesitation. Without a shadow of doubt, I believe Atala allowed this to happen. I can only hope that one day we will know why.

After Atala's death, the kingdom was thrust into a state of chaos. Brother fought against brother for decades in what the people called the **Dragon Wars**!

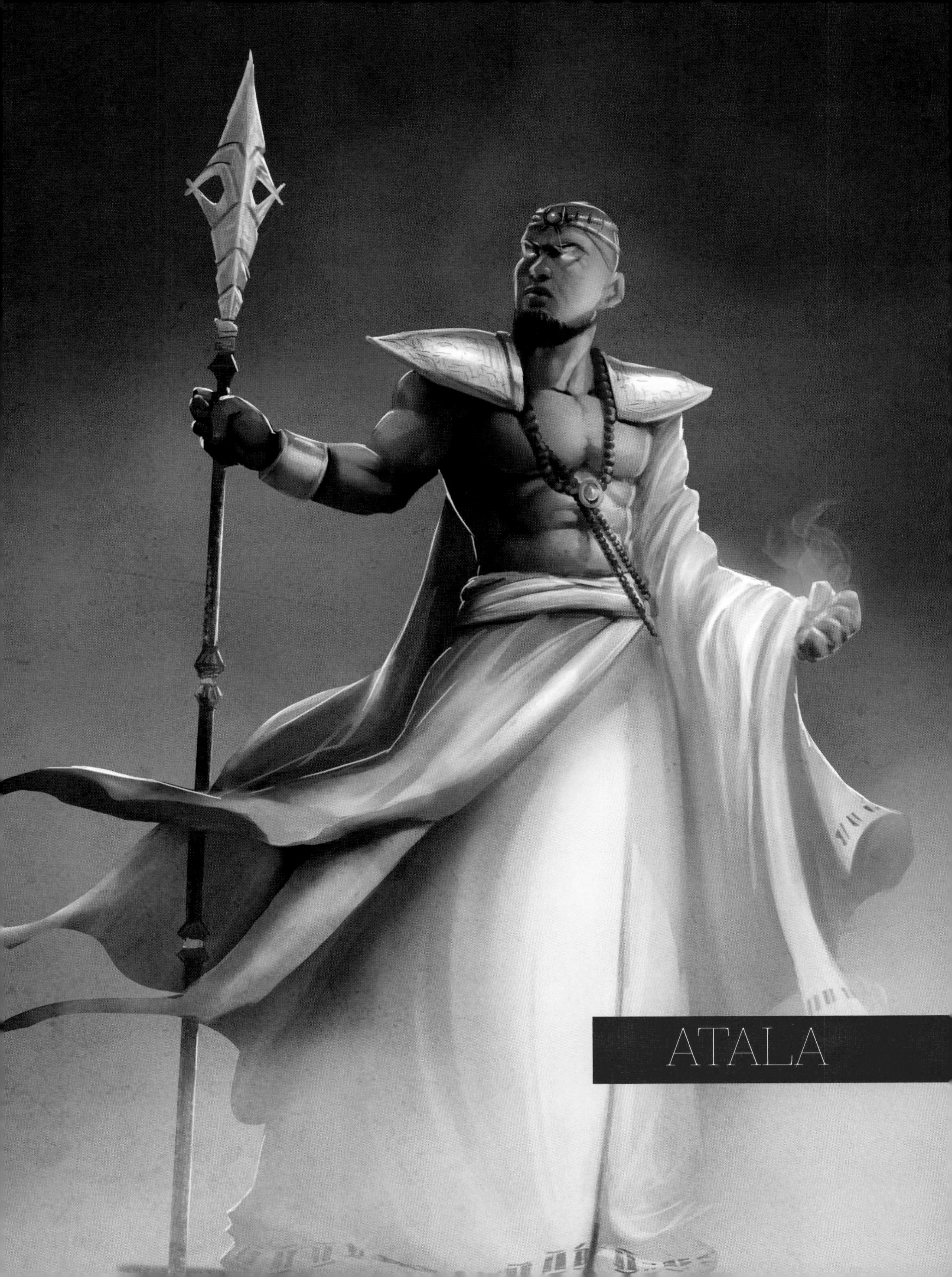

ATALA

Atala - The First Father

Atala is the most powerful being that has ever existed. No one truly knows his origin or how he came to be. It is said in certain texts that he descended directly from the **Skies of Dumar**, via the **Olof Conduit**. In his prime, Atala was a loving, fair and just ruler. A king who constantly put the desires of his subjects above his. A sovereign who would gladly die to bear the burdens of even his lowest subject. Wondu the Wise, high priest of Atala probably said it best: "A better leader there never was."

Until his bitter son killed him. Heartless traitor. How selfish and evil you are, Useh. Constantly favoring your greed and lust for power over peace and tranquility. But I digress. Atala's period of rule was famously called **The Time of Dragons**. He was the first to ever ride and subdue these formidable beasts, who were said to have been birthed by the elements of life.

Useh - The Prince of Rage

Never has one being harbored so much darkness and evil. From birth, Useh was always the jealous one and his thirst for power did him no good, as he mischievously tried to win over the affection of Atala. When it was clear his tactics weren't working, Useh killed his own father with a weapon forged from pure rage.

After Useh channeled his rage into tremendous power, he recruited many who had similar feelings of hatred, vengeance, anger and fear. And the world has no shortage of such people.

While researching the Dragon Wars, I came across dozens of pages missing from several texts. Some believe these missing pages were deliberately ripped from the collection to hide many of Useh's great atrocities. One of which was attempting to corrupt the **Archdragon**. A mythical beast said to only ever have bonded with Atala himself.

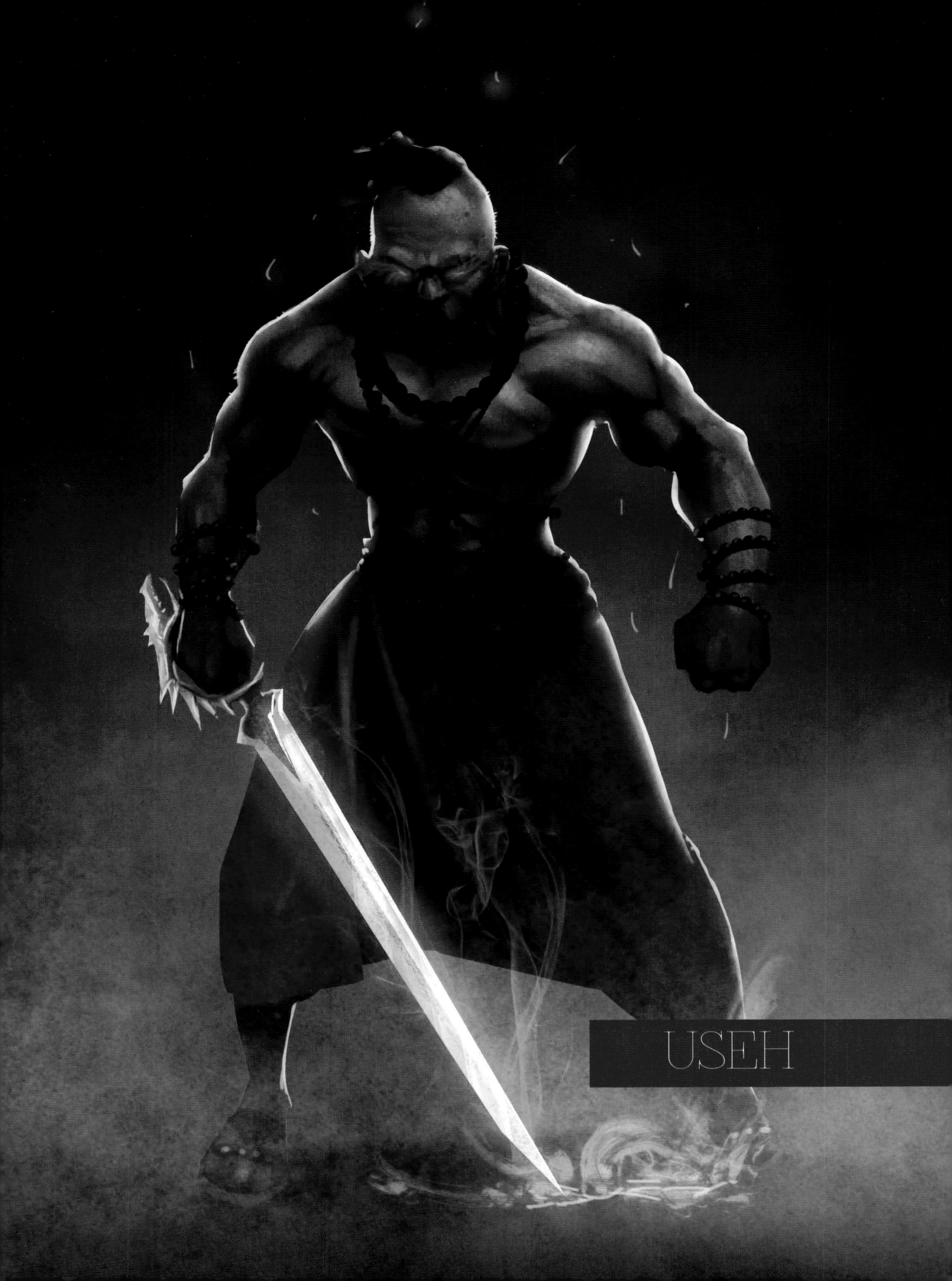

USEH

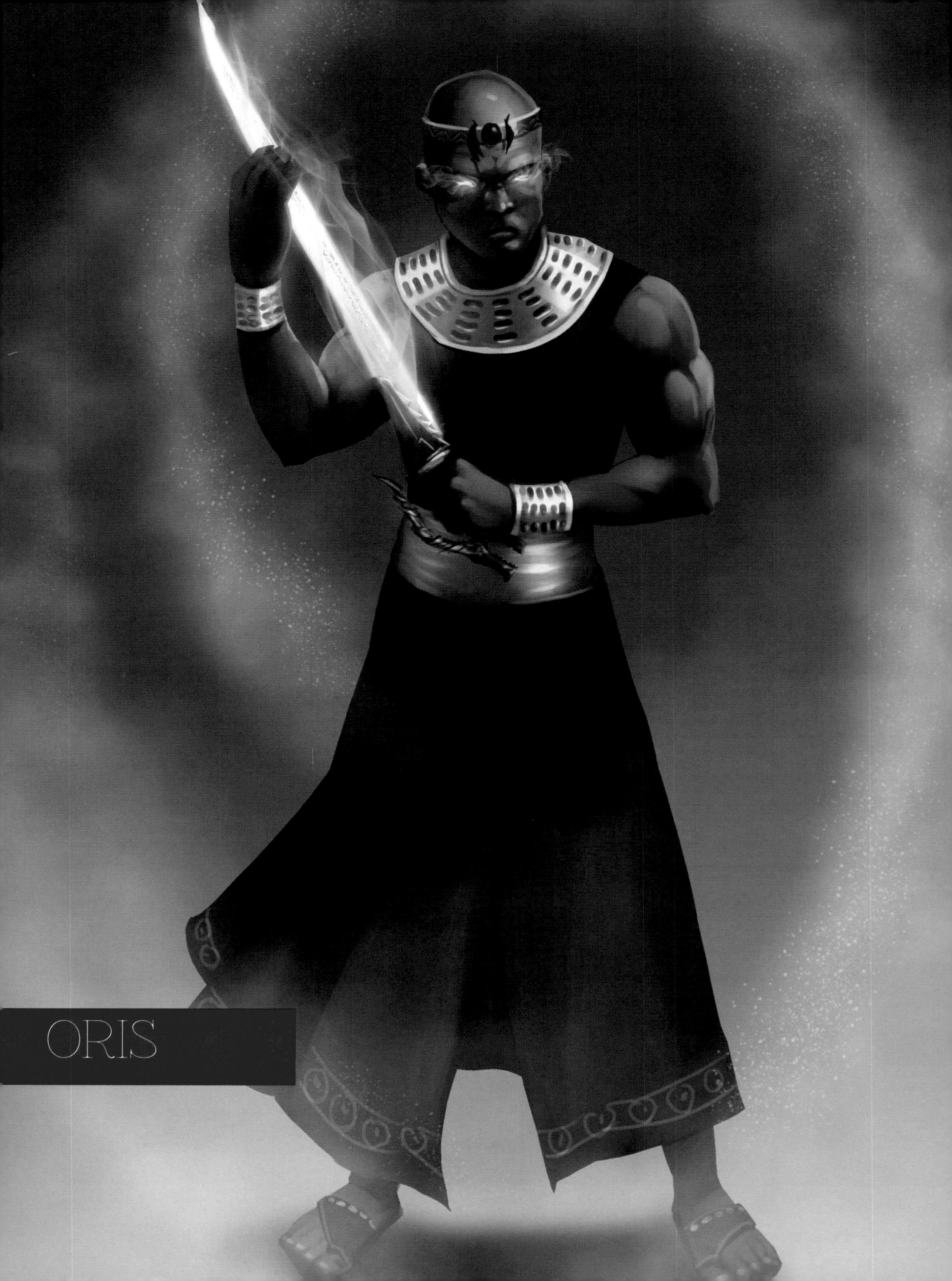
ORIS

Oris - The King of Light

From birth, Oris was the antithesis of his brother, Useh. Like his father, Oris was kind, fair and just, but possessed another trait that rose above all others: Compassion. On many occasions, Oris went out of his way to empathize with his mischievous brother. Incredibly wise, Oris was a prodigy from birth. Learning constantly from Atala, everything came to him with ease. This further drove Useh mad, despite the fact that Oris would spend much of his own personal time mentoring his struggling brother.

Once Useh killed Atala, however, it was clear that the battle lines were drawn. And though Oris still had great love for his fallen brother, he knew Useh had to be stopped. Years of bloody and grueling warfare commenced, and thousands of lives were lost. In time however, Oris, astute as ever, outsmarted his eager brother. He won the war, but defeating Useh left him with a severely broken heart. Seeing how the power of dragons had corrupted men, Oris hid both Dragon's Destiny and Dragon's Doom as well as converted the powers of each dragon into powerful stone relics.

Once order and peace were restored, Oris named this new united kingdom after his fallen father. And thus our nation became the **Kingdom of Atala**. Our flag forever honors The First Father, by having the first and last symbols of his name superimposed on each other, with the circle encompassing the symbols representing the lasting unity Oris hoped for.

I end this chapter with one of the famous quotes of Wondu. Never have I read something so frightening and comforting at the same time.

"A day will come when darkness will return. From the depths he will rise and we mortals will be the cause of his return. War, oppression, genocide, everything we have done to express our hatred for one another will empower him. But fear not, for light will return as well. And with light will come triumph. For light travels fastest in darkness."

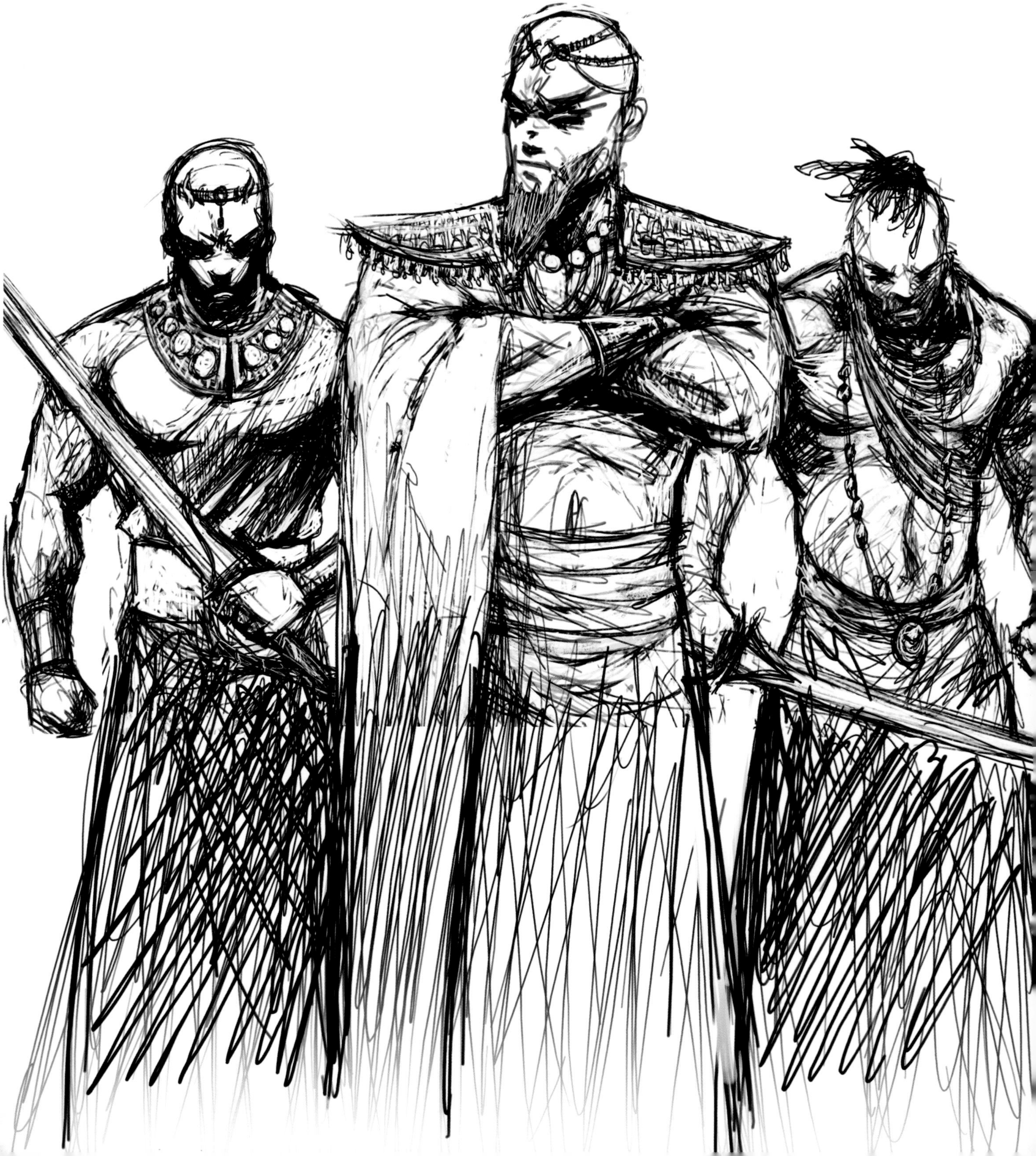

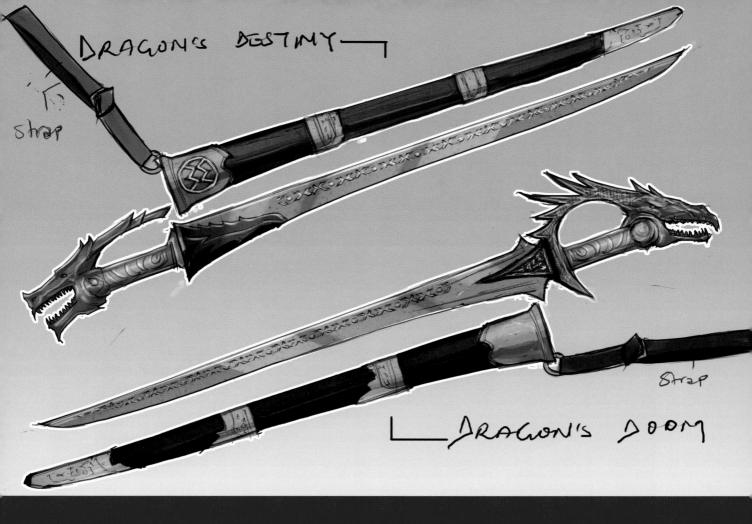

DRAGON'S DESTINY

Strap

Strap

DRAGON'S DOOM

"Harnessed from raw power, these relics were created from the most fundamental of opposites. One from light and the other from darkness."

Wondu The Wise

"For where there is light, darkness ceases to reign. The smallest of candlesticks can be spotted in a city of shadows"

King Bass Kazaar aka The WindMaker.

2
THE SWORDS

The **Dragon Swords** are two of the most powerful weapons ever crafted. Yet, as Wondu eloquently explained, their origin and purpose are completely opposite. Fearful that their powers would eventually corrupt men again, Oris hid both Dragon Swords. Following in his footsteps, Atalians have kept these powerful relics hidden from the world. A duty we failed to uphold after **General Cheng** of the **Ming Dynasty** got his hands on Dragon's Doom.

Dragon's Destiny

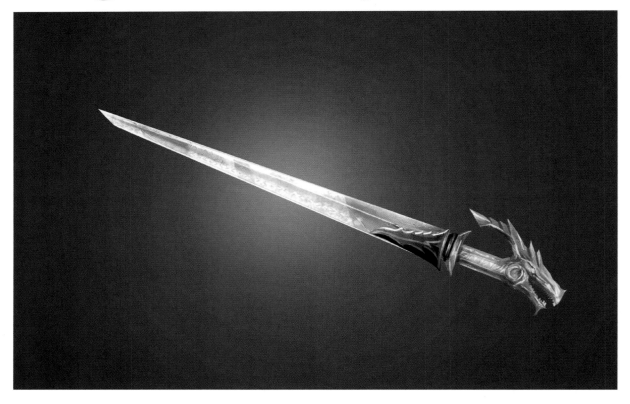

Crafted by Atala himself, this sword was created to be a beacon of hope for the people. Hope that the power of light will always consume that of darkness. Forged from the breath of dragons, Dragon's Destiny contains the very essence of each one of the magnificent creatures. Fire, Frost, Wind, Lightening and Water, all fused into the weapon to create unmatched power, a power that reigned supreme until the creation of Dragon's Doom.

Dragon's Doom

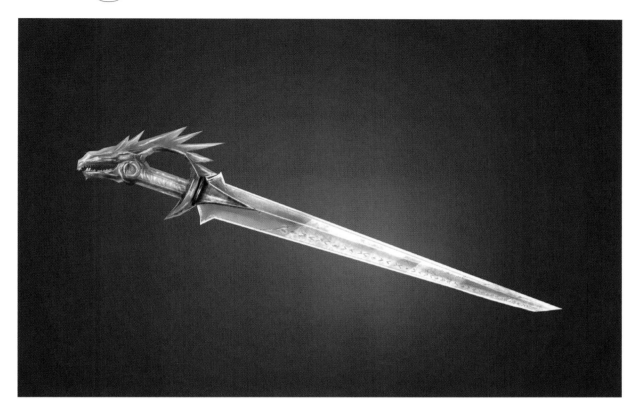

Rage, hatred, bitterness and vengeance. These are just some of the traits that give Dragon's Doom its powers. Since the beginning of time until now, no single being has harbored more of these traits than the Prince of Rage himself, Useh. Dragon's Doom was forged from the rage that consumed Useh after Dragon's Destiny was given to Oris. Its powers are seemingly limitless. The more the wielder of this ominous weapon harbors hate, rage and bitterness, the more powerful the sword becomes. Making it the most dangerous piece of weaponry ever crafted.

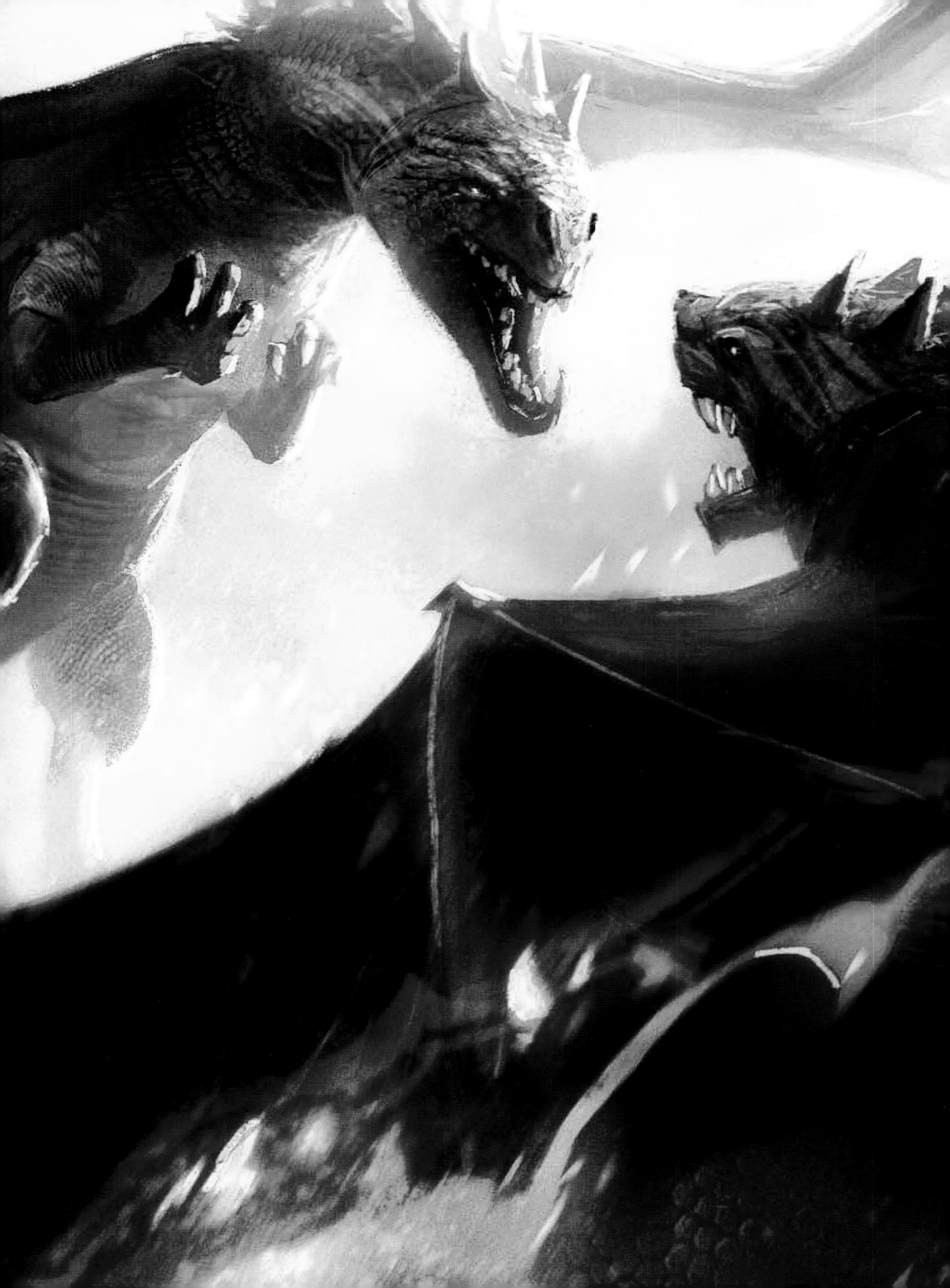

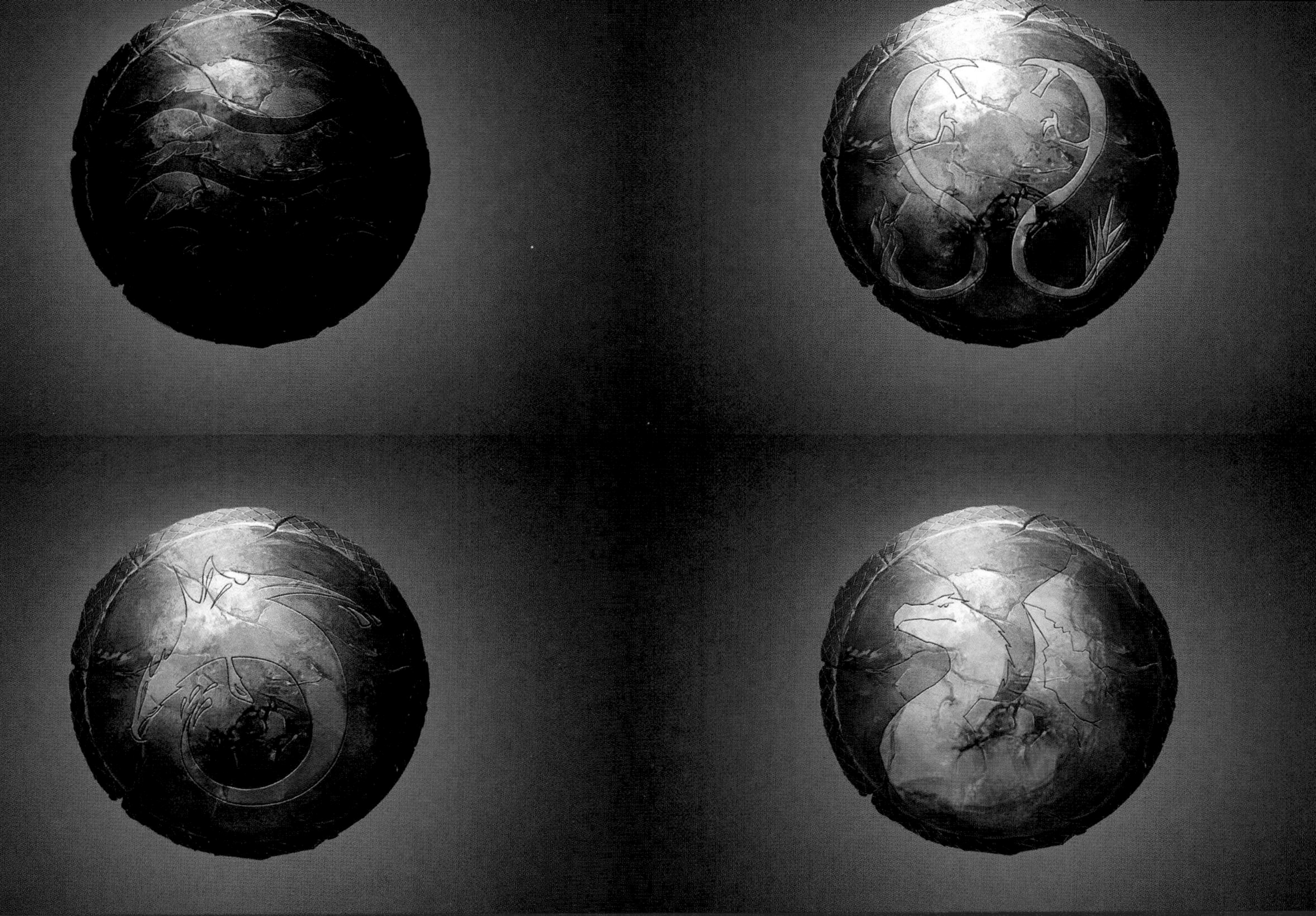

"A time will come when the treachery of absolute evil will doom us all. In that very moment, the beasts will rise from slumber. And twelve will stand with the light."

– Wondu The Wise

3

The Dragons

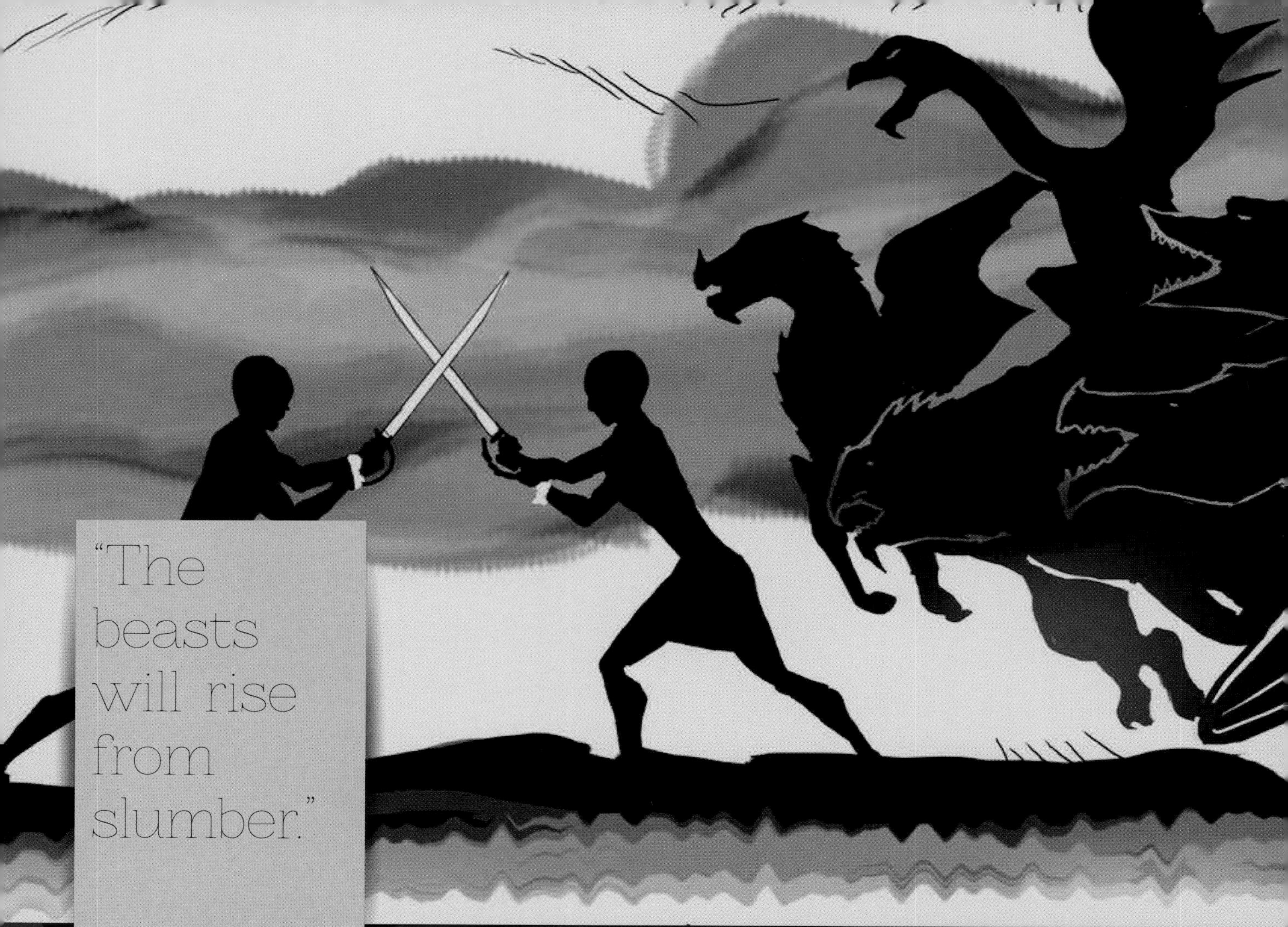

> "The beasts will rise from slumber."

Of all the research and scripts I have perused over the years, no subject's facts have eluded me quite like that of the Dragons and **Dragon Stones**. Vague texts, sketchy origins, and even pages ripped from the history books, trying to put together a solid and believable summary of these creatures has been a frustrating experience. No wonder the sages of old spoke in riddles about them. Nevertheless, I will provide as accurate of information as I possibly can. I do hope I can subdue the perfectionist within me while I do so.

"The five dragons were said to have manifested out of the elements of life."

From what I have gathered, there were five dragons and four dragon stones. However, there seems to be some very vague hints in the scripts that suggest a sixth dragon. Some call it the **Archdragon**. Apparently, it was a supremely powerful creature that only Atala himself could bond with. Whether or not it actually existed, no one knows.

The five dragons were said to have manifested out of the elements of life. But after the Dragon Wars, Oris had seen enough of how their powers corrupted men. So after he hid the Dragon Swords, he went a step further. The elders tell us that he condensed each dragon's power into what we now call the Stones of Oris. The Fire and Frost dragon share one stone. With their powers safely concealed, Oris sent each of the four stones to the different corners of the earth. As for the location of the dragons themselves, the elders simply tell us that they "vanished." Imprudent men. Could no one have recorded such important history back then? This is one of the most important aspects of Atalian history, yet no one thought to document it? Incredible. Fortunately, the texts do have records of the individual creatures when they were alive.

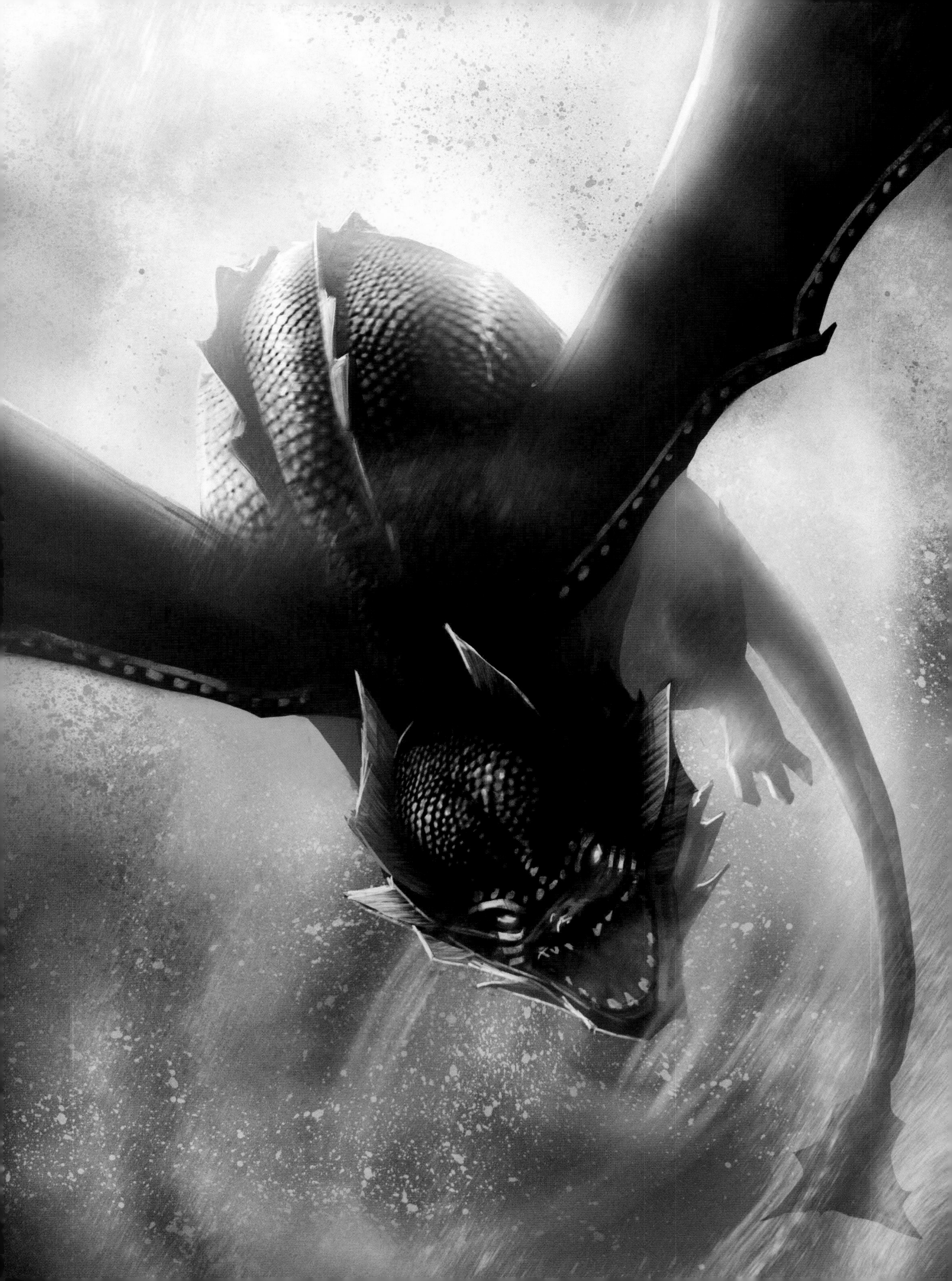

YAO - The Queen of Air

"She was able to heal at a remarkable rate."

When it comes to Atalian mythology, Yao is one of the most important. She shares the same powers with our King, the power to manipulate the wind. This black goddess is the fastest of all the dragons. History is littered with tales of how Yao regularly traversed the skies at unimaginable speeds. Speeds that caused the sky itself to crack and expel loud noises. Yao was said to also be a very wise beast.

Oris chose to conceal the **Wind Stone** in Atala, after condensing Yao's powers into it. He then sent the other three stones far away to the East, North and West. Many postulate that Oris hid the Wind Stone in Atala as a way to protect the Kingdom. It his hard to argue with their thinking when he wrote, "In the very likely chance that Atala needs a protector, the stone will call to the chosen one." Fortunately, our king located the Wind Stone before the treacherous general Cheng destroyed us all.

Each dragon was said to have a secondary trait that complemented its primary ability. For Yao, she was able to heal at a remarkable rate.

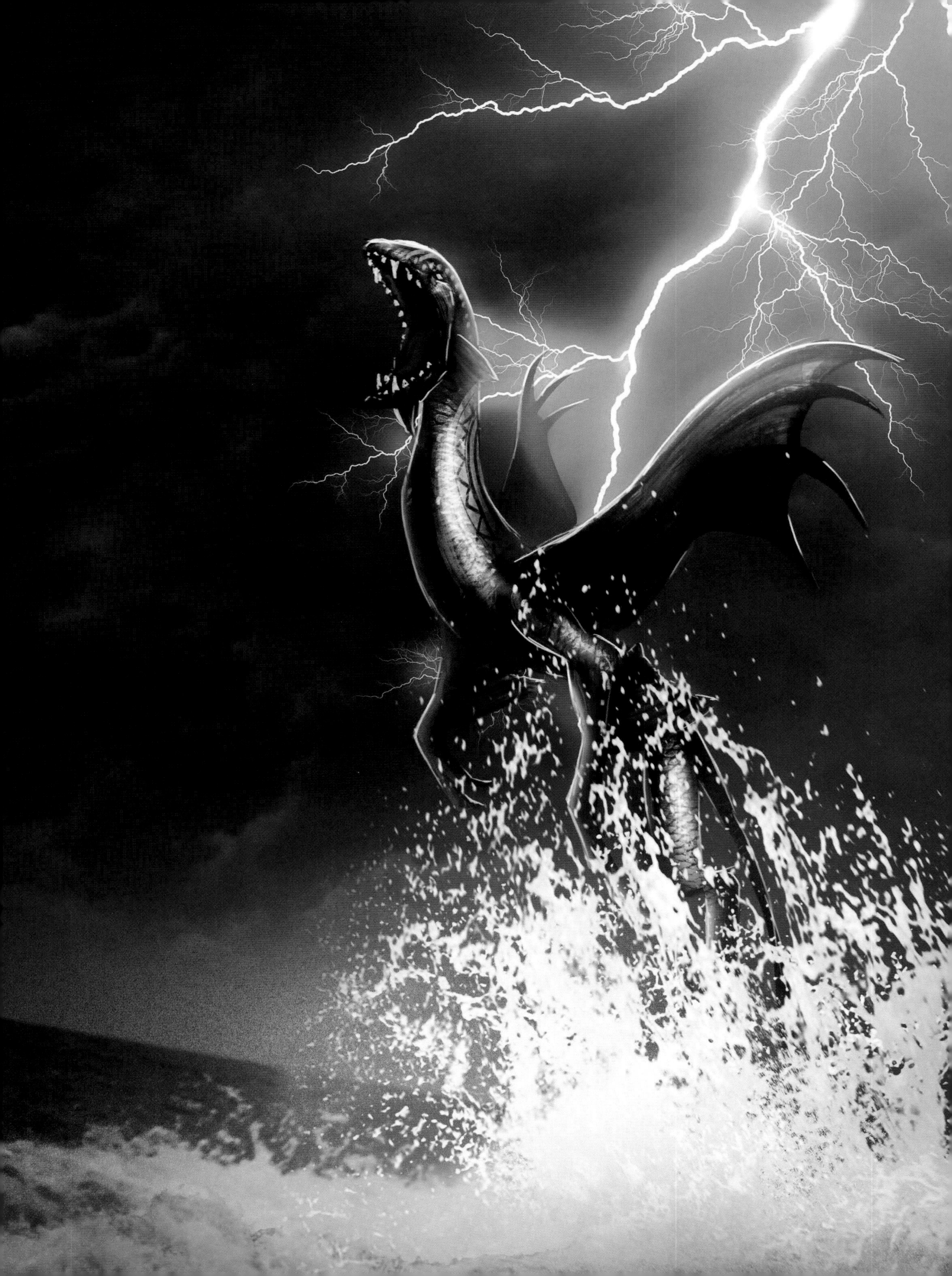

MOJA - The Mother of Oceans

"Moja's secondary traits were her heightened senses."

Moja was blessed with the ability to exploit the waves of the seas. She was the smallest of all the dragons, and one of the most tranquil. But when roused, she had the ability to be quite destructive and extremely violent, causing the most extreme of sea storms. Various accounts have Moja consuming entire settlements in one breath.

Eyewitnesses within Oris' court suggest that the three stones levitated towards the sky, then suddenly split into three directions, with the **Water Stone** cast west of the Aethiopian Sea, causing a mystical disruption in the ocean in that region.

Moja's secondary traits were her heightened senses. In addition to smelling, seeing and hearing farther than any living creature, she could also feel deeper. These abilities combined made it appear as if she could foresee an adversary's attacks.

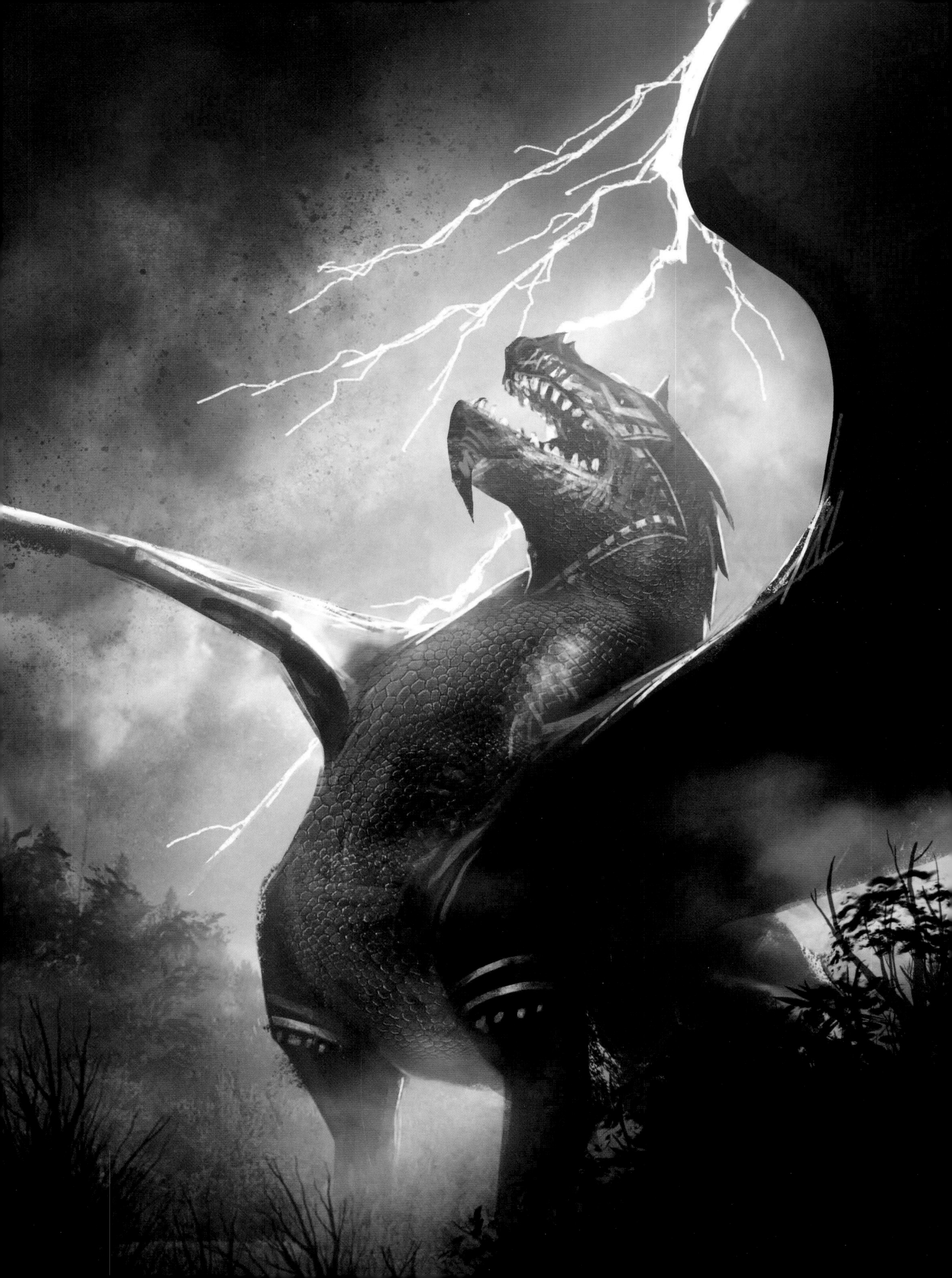

GANSO - - The Shock Behemoth

"The very
earth
trembled
as Ganso
made his
approach."

Ganso is the dragon of lightning. The largest and strongest of all the dragons, the very earth trembled as Ganso made his approach. Extremely witty, he was also temperamental, though not the most temperamental of all the dragons. As with the Water Stone, the **Lightning Stone** was also thrust far away by Oris. But to the north of Atala. Ganso's secondary trait was his extraordinary strength.

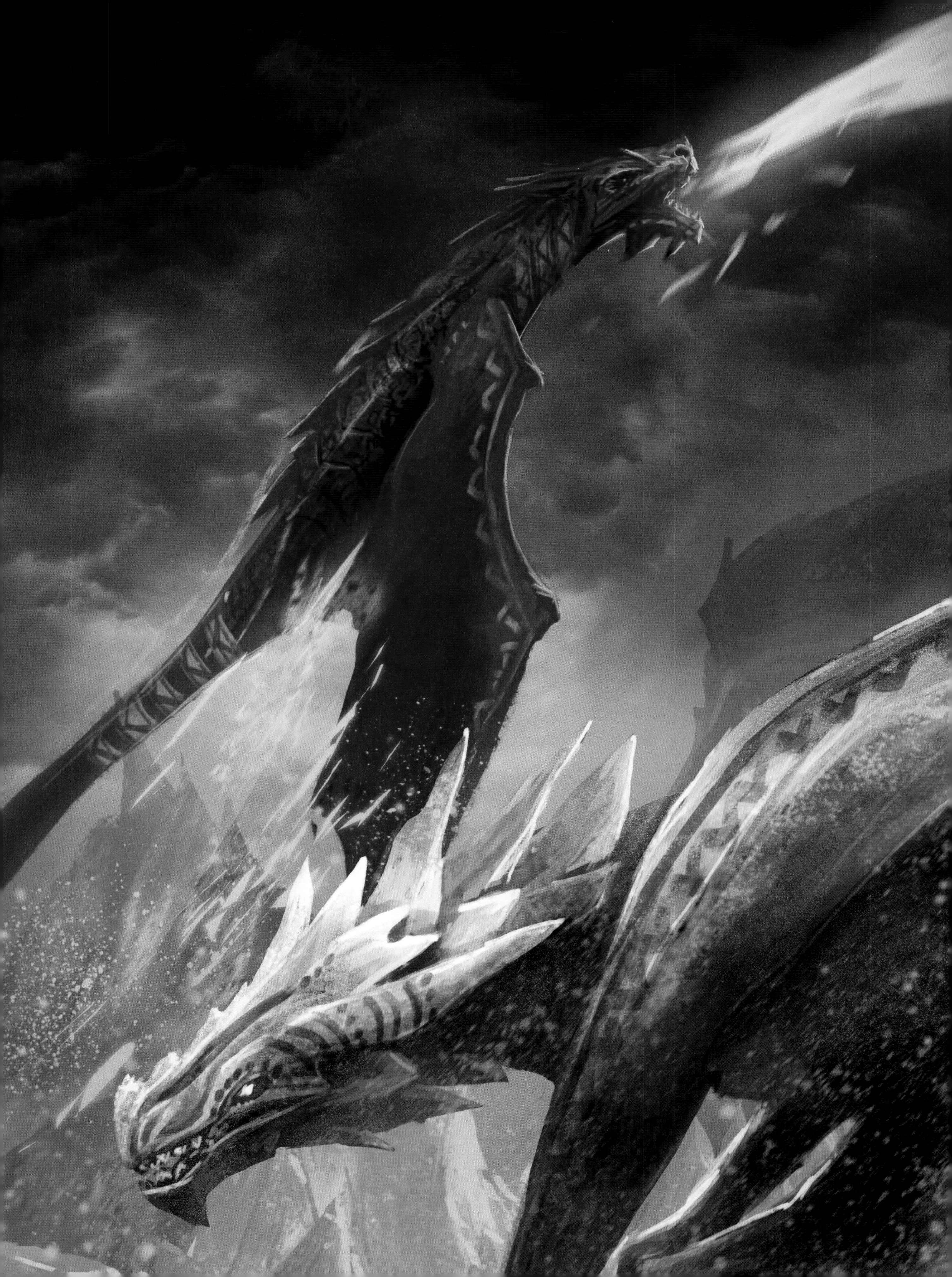

BEJI - The Twin Dragons

e **Twin Dragons**, or **Ibeji** as my people call them, are truly inseparable creatures. The
eji are considered one soul contained in two dragons. This is further evidenced by the
aim that if one dies so does the other. As inseparable as the sacred texts tell us these
asts were, I find it quite amusing the differences in their individual comportments.

ANJU - The Fire Dragon

as not expecting a creature with the ability to breath fire to be the most peaceful of beasts,
t by the skies of Dumar, the accounts of Ganju are terrifying. As a young clerk studying
e scripts, I read an account where Ganju once went on a rampage, burning down several
lages because a town crier accidentally disturbed his slumber. It was such a horrifying
ent that Atala himself had to intervene and subdue the beast. What a savage animal! He
arly was the most temperamental of all the dragons.

anju also constantly picked fights with his twin sister **Okun**, the very thing he loved the
ost. I supposed it does help that they both had near **unbreakable skin** as their secondary
ait.

KUN - The Frost Dragon

e complete opposite of her twin brother, Okun is the most reserved and level-headed of
l the dragons. She was the hardest to gather information about, as many descriptions were
gue. If I were to rely solely on tales I heard as a child, she was said to be very mysterious,
ten distancing herself from the other dragons except Ganju. Just like her twin brother
anju, the texture of her skin was near unbreakable, except she also had several protruding
ards around her body, making it virtually impossible for any foe to deal damage at close
oximity.

ris condensed the powers of the forever-inseparable Ibeji into a single stone. The stone
as thrust towards the east of Atala.

hus concludes the bemusing tale of the legendary dragons and the dragon stones. But as
ith every bewildering story, there is one more mystery to these magnificent creatures.
egend has it that whomever comes in contact with these stones will be, "blessed with the
ower of dragons." As one who relies heavily on research and factual evidence, I scoffed at
is very notion, until I saw it manifest right before my very eyes as my king became **The
indMaker**.

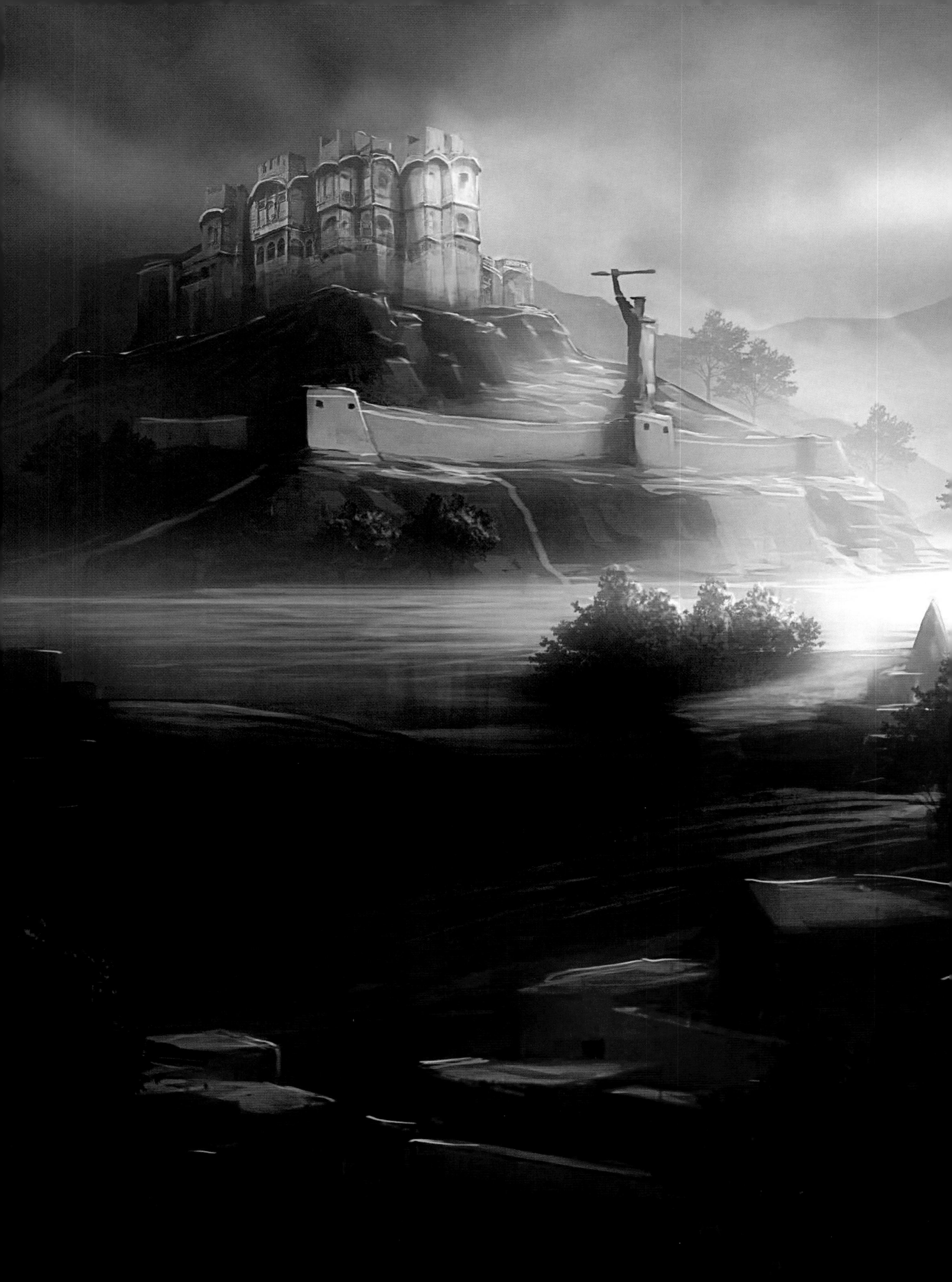

"To believe you must have faith and to have
faith you must believe."

Wondu The Wise

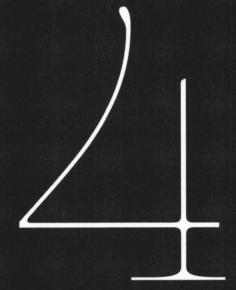

4
THE GREAT MIGRATION

The one question many have about the First Father, Atala, is where exactly did he come from? I made this very query to several sages and none could quite give me an accurate account. I assume telling a vague story is preferable to admitting you know not the answer to an important question. It may appear as if I am mocking the wise ones in charge of safekeeping the knowledge of our precepts, and maybe even doubting the teachings. But I assure you it is quite the opposite. I am steadfast in my beliefs pertaining to our history, culture and heritage, despite its many deviations from facts. Sometimes my practicality interferes with my beliefs. This is where faith comes in. For how can one believe, except without faith.

After settling in the **Oyo Kingdom**, Atala took the love of his life, Maya, as his wife. They had two sons Oris and Useh. **Awudu** was Atala's ambitious younger brother. For one cannot tell the story of the great migration without telling the story of Awudu. Sent to earth after him, Awudu was motivated by conquest and a desire for control. Over the years, it became clear to Atala that both he and his brother could no longer coexist. Rather than wage war with blood, Atala, ever the benevolent one, left the Oyo Kingdom.

Thus began the great migration south towards Atala's new kingdom, a kingdom that would eventually be named after him.

"The ease of peace is a prerequisite to loss in war."

Wondu The Wise

5

THE GREAT INVASION

MING

The Ming Dynasty is the ruling empire of China that followed the demise of the Yuan Dynasty. With its capital in Beijing, the Ming Dynasty boasts one of the most organized governments and socially stable economies.

The invasion of **General Cheng** and the **Ming Dynasty** was the beginning of the darkest period in Atalian history. After Oris' death and up until the invasion, we Atalians were a very peaceful nation. During that period, we did not even believe in the concept of having an army. Of course looking back, that was a very foolish notion.

It all started after the demise of Oris. In the long history of our great nation, there have only been three kings. Atala, Oris, and centuries later, our current king, Bass Kazaar. Oris left no heirs, so after his death, our nation became an oligarchy, or more specifically Gerontocracy. The elders ruled as a committee. Paranoid from the dragon wars, the elders constantly preached peace and unity. Passed down from generation to generation, it became the Atalian mantra. But the issue with focusing on peace is that it makes you unprepared for war. And war was coming.

The Ming Dynasty

The Ming Dynasty is the ruling empire of China that followed the demise of the Yuan Dynasty. With its capital in Beijing, the Ming Dynasty boasts one of the most organized governments and socially stable economies. An army of over a million troops makes the Ming Dynasty the most formidable force in the world. Of course, our elders knew none of this when the Ming army first docked on our shores. In their own words, they came as "peaceful explorers of world trade." Of course we now know they were after our most prized possessions, the Dragon Swords and Stones.

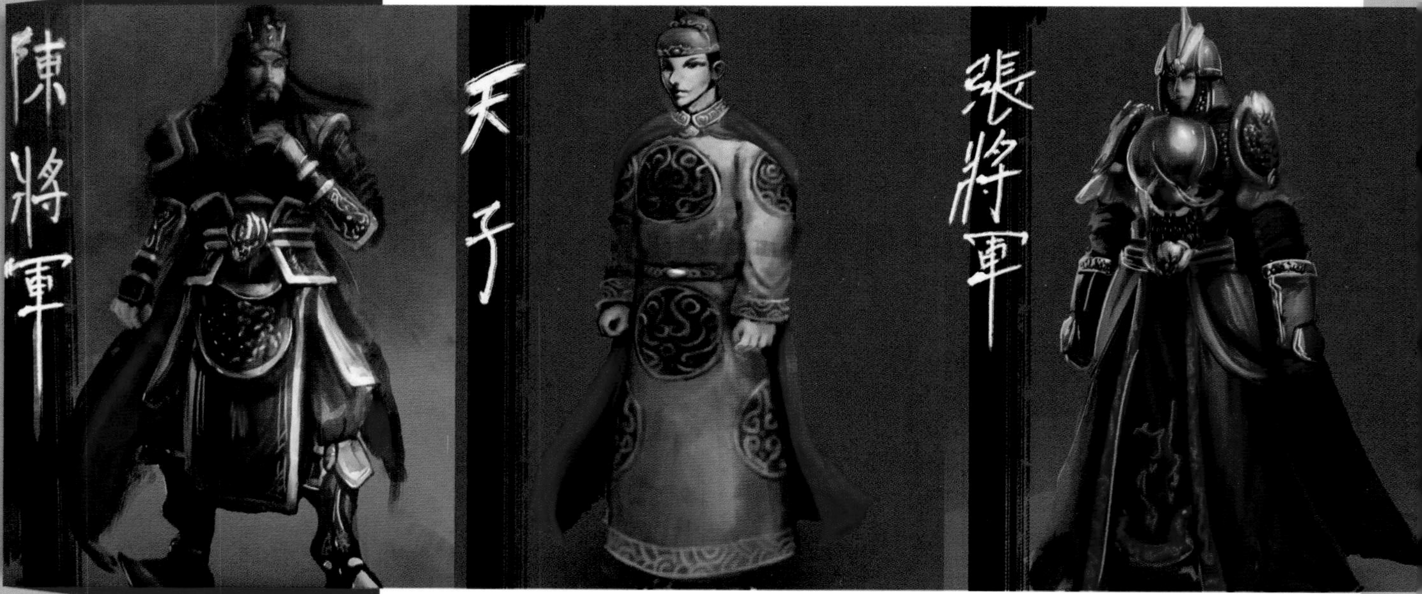
陳將軍
天子
張將軍

Spearheading this expedition was none other than renowned military commander, General Cheng.

General Cheng

I am fully convinced that this wretch of a man has no soul. He is evil incarnate, a demon who is constantly on the prowl to conquer and subjugate worlds, a warmonger who goes about waging war in the most despicable of ways. Ever the cunning fiend, Cheng took advantage of our elder's generous hospitality and naivety. Under the guise of, "trade and exchange of information," Cheng seduced our elders into trusting him more and more. And the more they trusted him, the further inland they welcomed him and his armies. The further inland he came, the more secrets he unraveled about our sacred relics.

It wasn't long before Cheng repaid their trust with treachery. Like an eagle circling the skies, Cheng waited for the perfect moment to strike. And when he did, his deadly claws ripped through our entire leadership. In a matter of days, the elders were destroyed and Cheng seized control of our kingdom and claimed his first prize, Dragon's Doom. But that was not enough to satisfy his thirst for our powerful relics. Next, he set his eyes on Dragon's Destiny and the rest of the Dragon Stones. Fortunately, there was one that dared to stand against Cheng's tyranny. Bass Kazaar, our king.

KUNG FU

The monk's martial arts technique or Kung Fu as they call it, was one of the most graceful and yet potent fighting styles I had ever witnessed at the time.

Even as a teenager, Bass was wise beyond his years. He outsmarted an entire regimen of Ming troops, securing Dragon's Destiny before they could. Angered by this, General Cheng concentrated his efforts on killing Bass, hoping to quell any ray of hope we Atalians had. And thus began the **Atalian rebellion**, a rebellion whose success would rely heavily on members of general Cheng's camp.

Master Yu and the Shaolin Monks

In the years following General Cheng's takeover, he built a series of temples on **Raven Island** for the monks who accompanied him to Atala. Originally, I had made up my mind that all who were from Ming were pure evil. But these men were different. And for a while the reasons puzzled me. At the order of **Master Yu**, leader of the monks, they never interfered in the matters of Ming and instead were content to simply practice their martial arts in peace. This caused a continuous friction between Cheng and Yu, with Cheng constantly questioning why the monks ever journeyed with him in the first place. But these monks had a code that they valued even higher than the orders of their general. The avoidance of violence. And no one embodied this ritual more than master Yu himself.

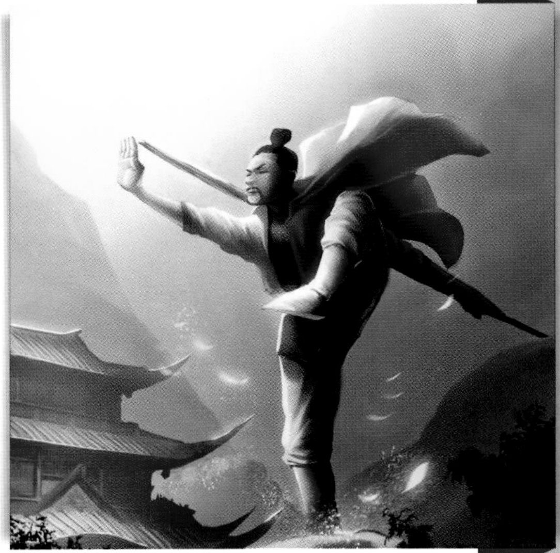

The monk's martial arts technique or **Kung Fu** as they call it, was one of the most graceful and yet potent fighting styles I had ever witnessed at the time. Though we Raven's now posses the skill and practice it religiously, it still amazes me how the monks constantly favored restraint over attacking prowess. However, if there was one thing the monks detested more than violence, it was violence inflicted upon innocents. For even though Shaolin Kung Fu preaches the avoidance of conflict, it also advocates that if an assailant is determined to cause harm, a more aggressive solution may be required. Master's Yu's solution to Cheng's oppression was to teach us the ancient arts of Kung Fu. The monks had grown tired of being idle as they witnessed the senseless massacre of a virtuous people. And if they could not fight for us against their kind, they were more than willing to teach us how to effectively fight back to defend ourselves.

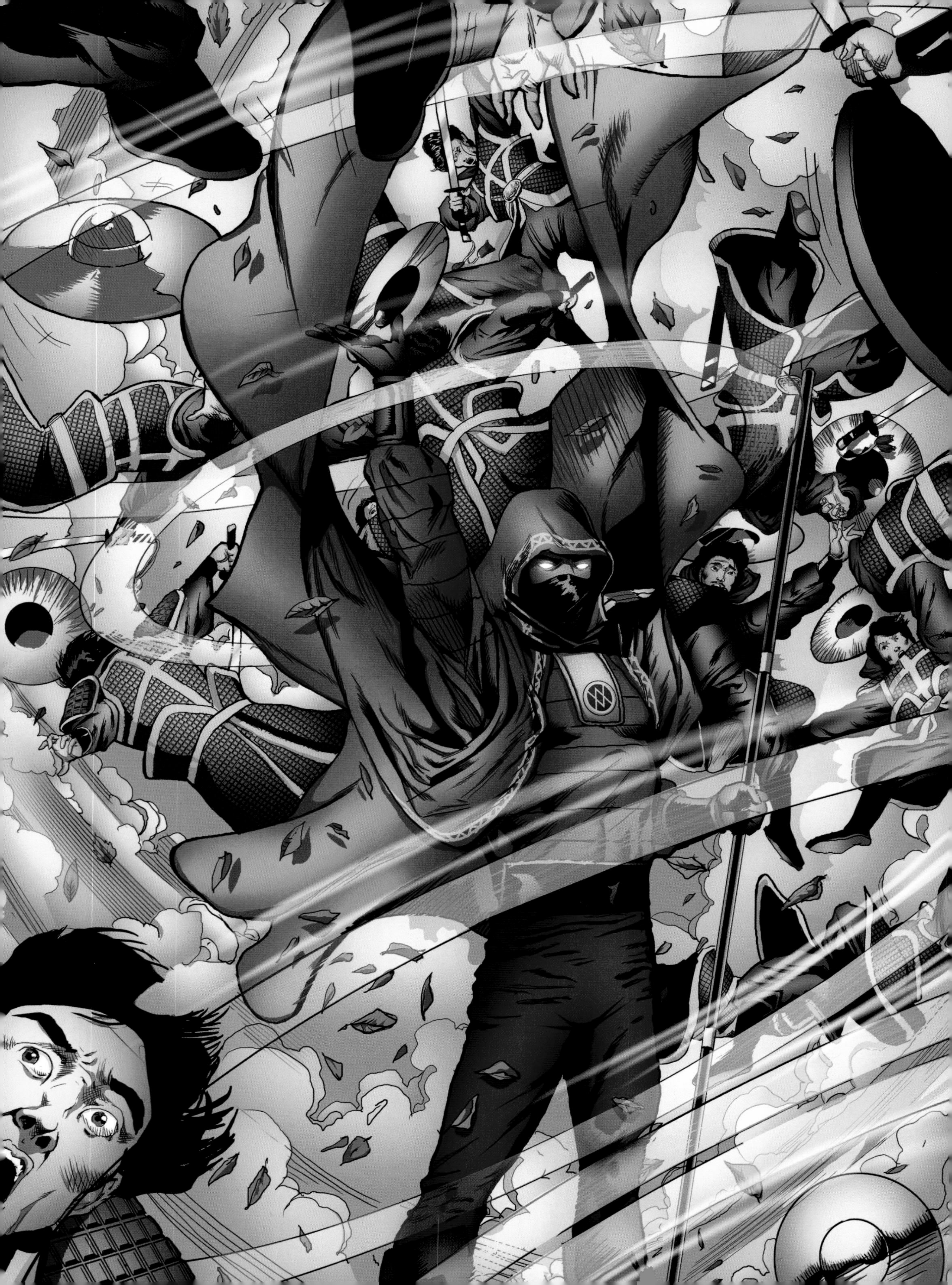

"Even the most peaceful of creatures can rise up to resist the chains oppression."

- Wondu The Wise

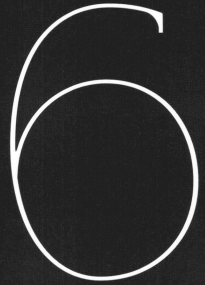

THE GREAT REVOLUTION

After Bass acquired Dragon's Destiny, Cheng focused a majority of his waking moments on capturing him. For years, Cheng searched for Bass without any success. He scoured the entire kingdom, but the one place he didn't think to search was the temples on Raven Island. For Cheng could not even fathom the possibility of a citizen of Ming associating with "barbarians," as he frequently called us. By the time he discovered the Monk's betrayal, it was too late.

The Red Ravens

Before he could be captured by Cheng, Bass fled Raven Island. But not before mastering the art of Shaolin Kung Fu. However, before Kung Fu, Bass trained in the ancient Atalian martial arts called **Olon-Jin**. A fighting style created by our ancestors which features acrobatic dodges, kicks and leg sweeps. After completing his training with Master Yu, Bass combined both Kung Fu and Olon-Jin into a singular style he would then teach those of us that wished to resist and take back our lands. We called ourselves the **Red Ravens**.

The small island southwest Island due to the large **Ravens** that lived high up slaughtered our elders, he in the open for all to see. descended to feast upon the Bass was one of the few close enough to witness upon the flesh of our elders' on their necks became To honor our fallen heroes, fought back for freedom For these birds now carried

Our Rebellion

I was one of the first to be only took a few words from after winning the fight the moment we decide to divinities, our king can of the Red Ravens, Bass of Kung Fu as we wandered avoiding General Cheng. We until Bass was convinced the to us. And the moment it

"We do not become free after winning the fight for freedom, we become free the moment we decide to fight for freedom."

Bass Kazaar. The King of Atala

of Atala was named Raven population of **White Necked** in the mountains. After Cheng left their bodies outside to rot Days went by as the Ravens flesh of our deceased elders. Atalians who bravely snuck this horror. As the Ravens fed carcasses, the white patches drenched blood, turning it red. Bass named us, the group that and justice, the Red Ravens. the souls of our fallen leaders.

recruited as a Raven. And it Bass. We do not become free for freedom, we become free fight for freedom. Blessed inspire a corpse! As leader drilled us for years in the art from settlement to settlement did not lift a fist against Ming art had become second nature did, we became unstoppable.

What followed was guerilla warfare at it's best. After all, we knew the lands more than Cheng and we used that to our advantage. We surprised Cheng and his captains with ambushes and forced them into battles in tight spaces, where their size counted for nothing. Over the years, little by little, their numbers dwindled. And the more Cheng lost, the more reckless he became. His frustrations lead him to abandon strategy and favor impatience. Bass, wiser than ever, baited Cheng into a final battle that favored us even though Cheng still had us outnumbered. With help from our **Azzazian** allies and their ferocious cavalry, we dealt the final blow. Cheng was beaten. But being the coward that he is, he fled Atala with the rest of his troops.

Following our victory, Bass was crowned king of Atala. The first since the King of Light himself, Oris. Any other mortal would have reveled in glory of such an outstanding achievement. Not my king. For he knew that as long as a monster like Cheng was alive and out there, Atala and her precious relics would never be safe. And thus began the plan to pursue Cheng and why we currently find ourselves here on foreign lands, chasing a demon.

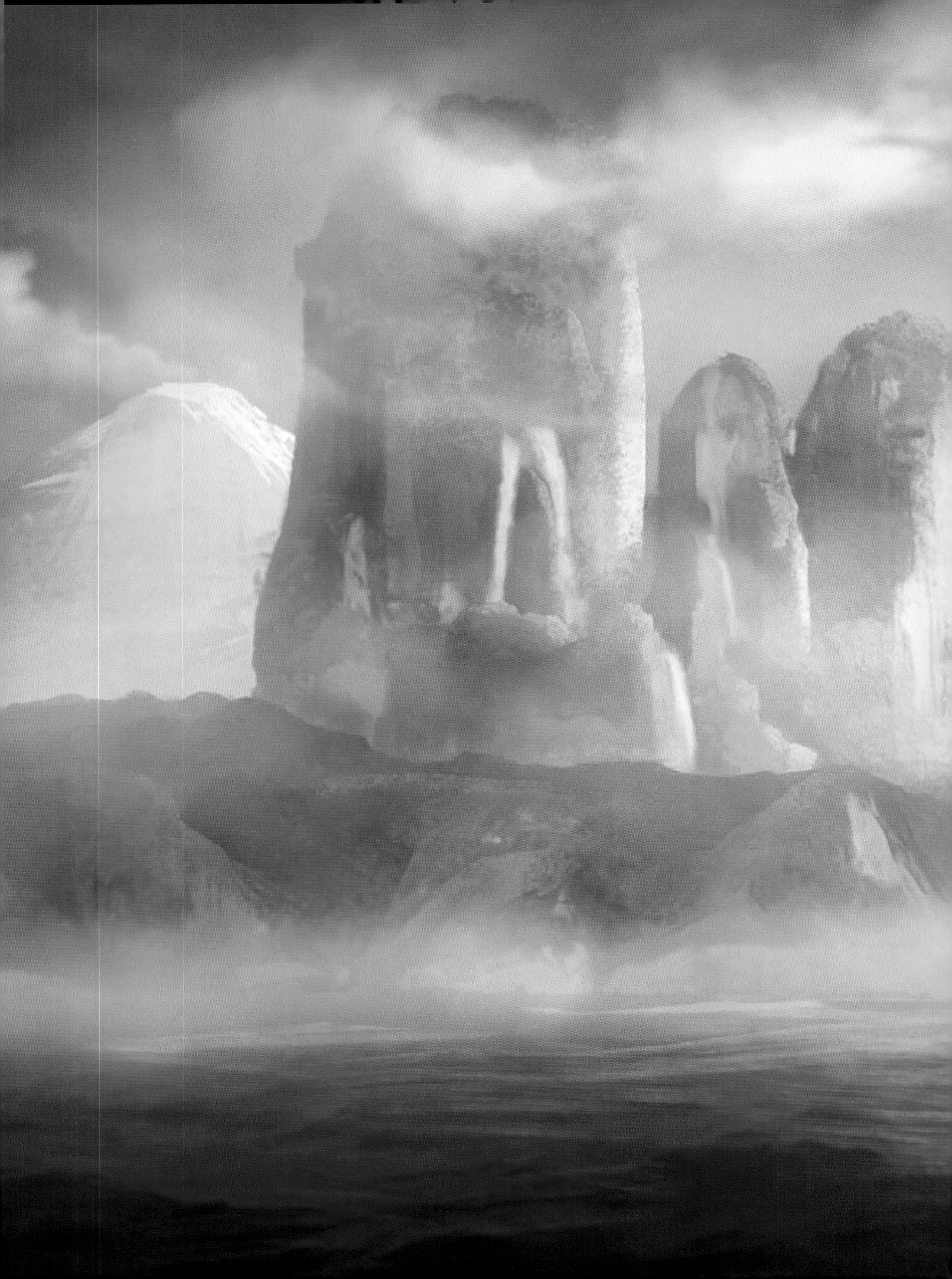

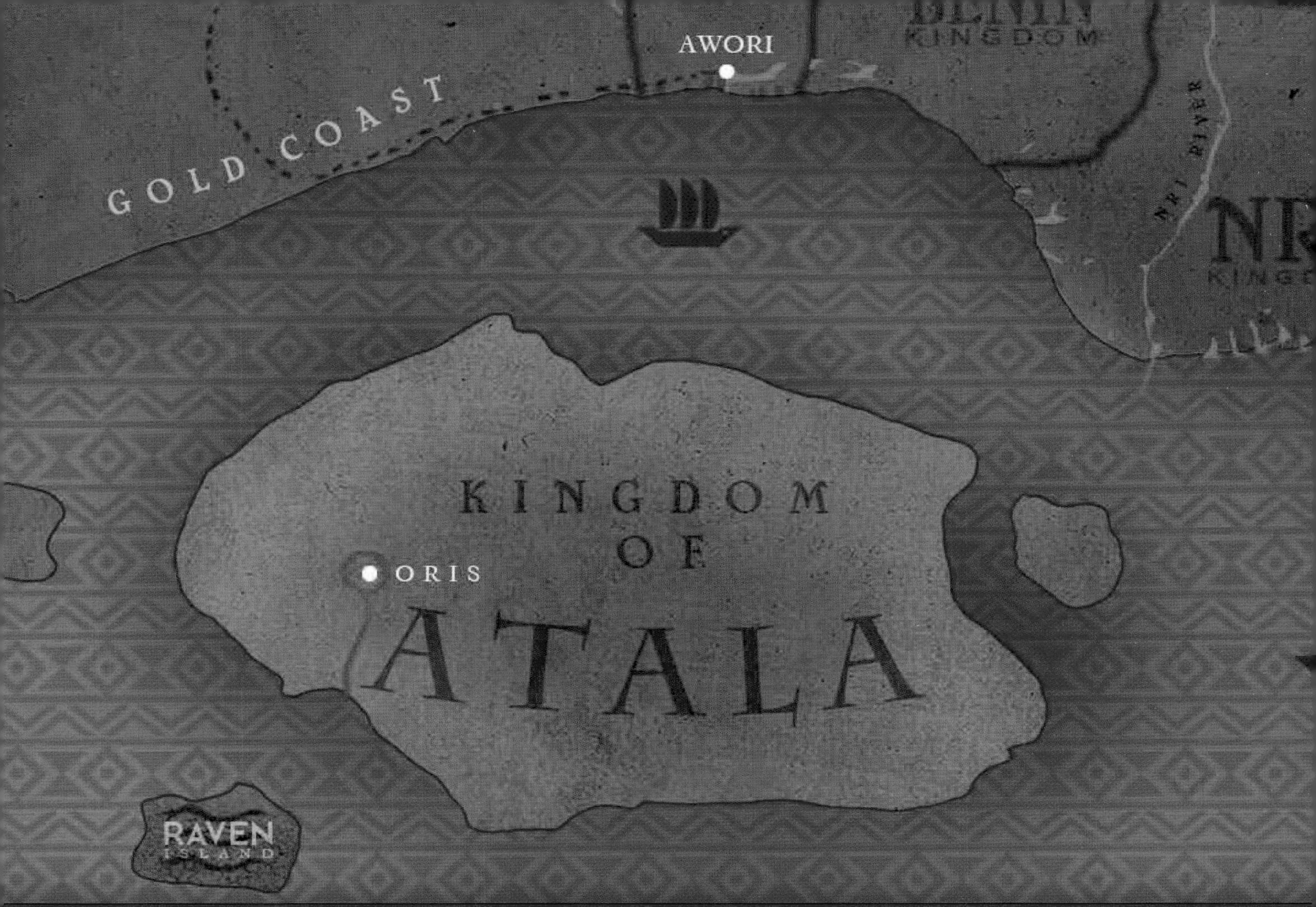
AWORI
BENIN
KINGDOM
GOLD COAST
NRI RIVER
KINGDOM OF ATALA
ORIS
RAVEN
ISLAND

"I will give my last breath to preserve the beauty of this great nation."

- Bass Kazaar, The WindMaker & King of Atala

7 The Islands

I imagine that in the future, when the shades of war have passed on, the great islands surrounding our great kingdom will be a lure for visitors from all over the world. Each one, equally as breathtaking as the next, is truly a wonder to behold. Raven Island

Raven Island

Raven Island was home to our elders, the leaders of old. An island where Atala himself frequently meditated, it was and still is considered holy ground. However, the most noticeable of elements currently on Raven Island are the Shaolin temples. Many questioned why our king did not simply destroy these last reminders of our Ming oppressors. But like other things many saw as doom, our king chose to find the light in it. These temples were a reminder of an important ally in the war for freedom, the monks. Our king did not only chose to preserve the temples, he encouraged many to learn the art of Shaolin Kung Fu. And until this very day, that knowledge is much a part of our history, as is the ancient martial arts of our ancestors, which Bass integrated into his trainings.

Forbidden Island

No one knows why, when or by whom, but the Forbidden Island is cursed. No human has set foot on the island and lived to tell the tale. An account from the ancient texts mentions that those who set foot on the island age so rapidly that they die in a matter of seconds.

One theory that many Atalians favor is that Oris hid the Wind Stone on the island, placing a curse over it to keep it safe. It would explain why the island is rumored to be riddled with bones. One can only imagine that many have tried to brave the curse to retrieve one of the most powerful relics ever created. However, our king recovering the Wind Stone put an end to that claim.

Island of the Frost

Home to the highest mountains known to man, the Island of the Frost is a sight to behold. In a way, it is a mountain protruding out of the ocean with mountains on it. Which is why it is also commonly referred to as the "mountain of mountains." At such a high elevation, the freezing temperatures are unbearable for most life forms. Making it the perfect home for the Frost Dragon during the time of dragons.

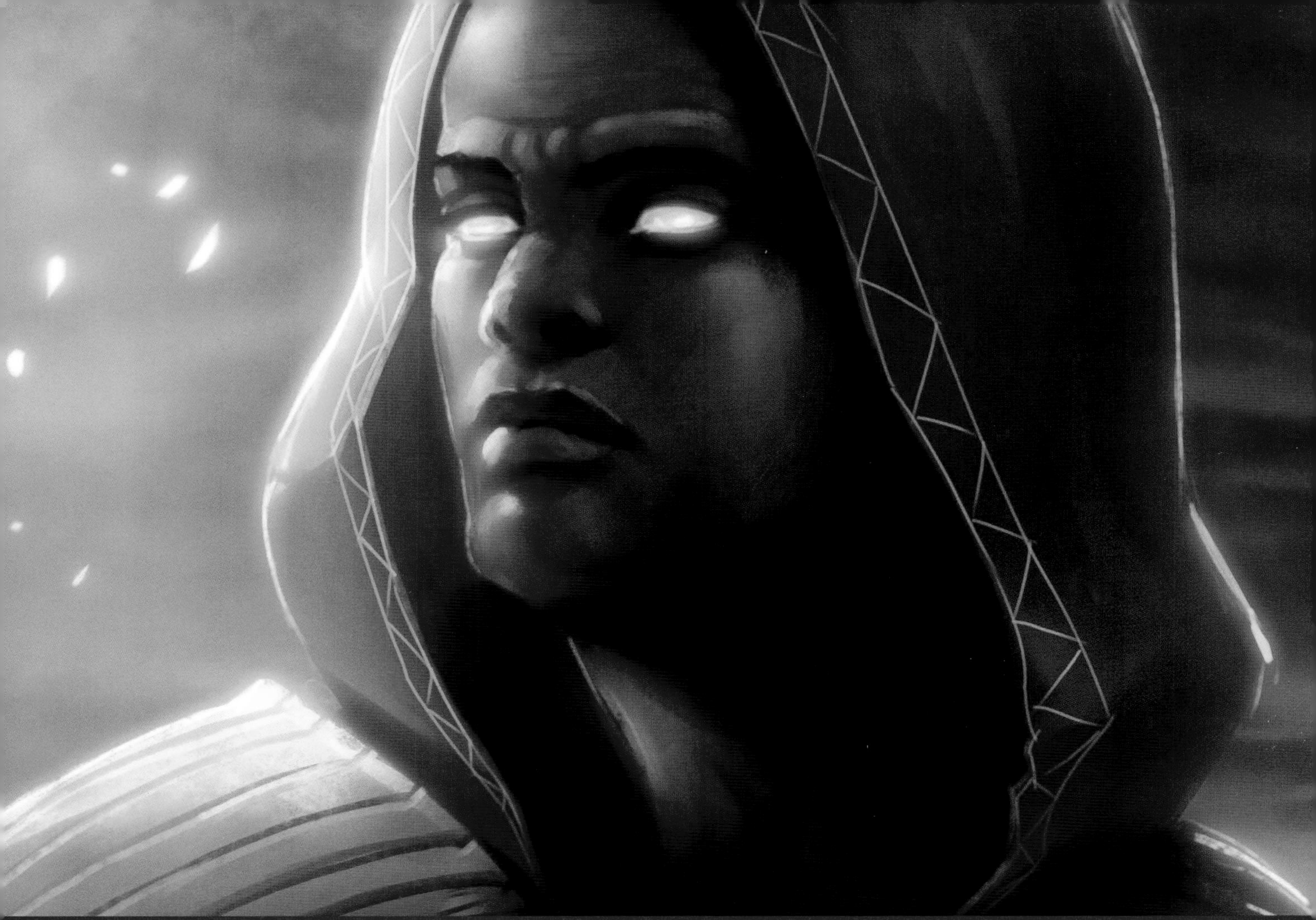

"Power in its infinite forms is simply a tool that should be used to serve the people."

- Bass Kazaar, The WindMaker & King of Atala

8
The WindMaker

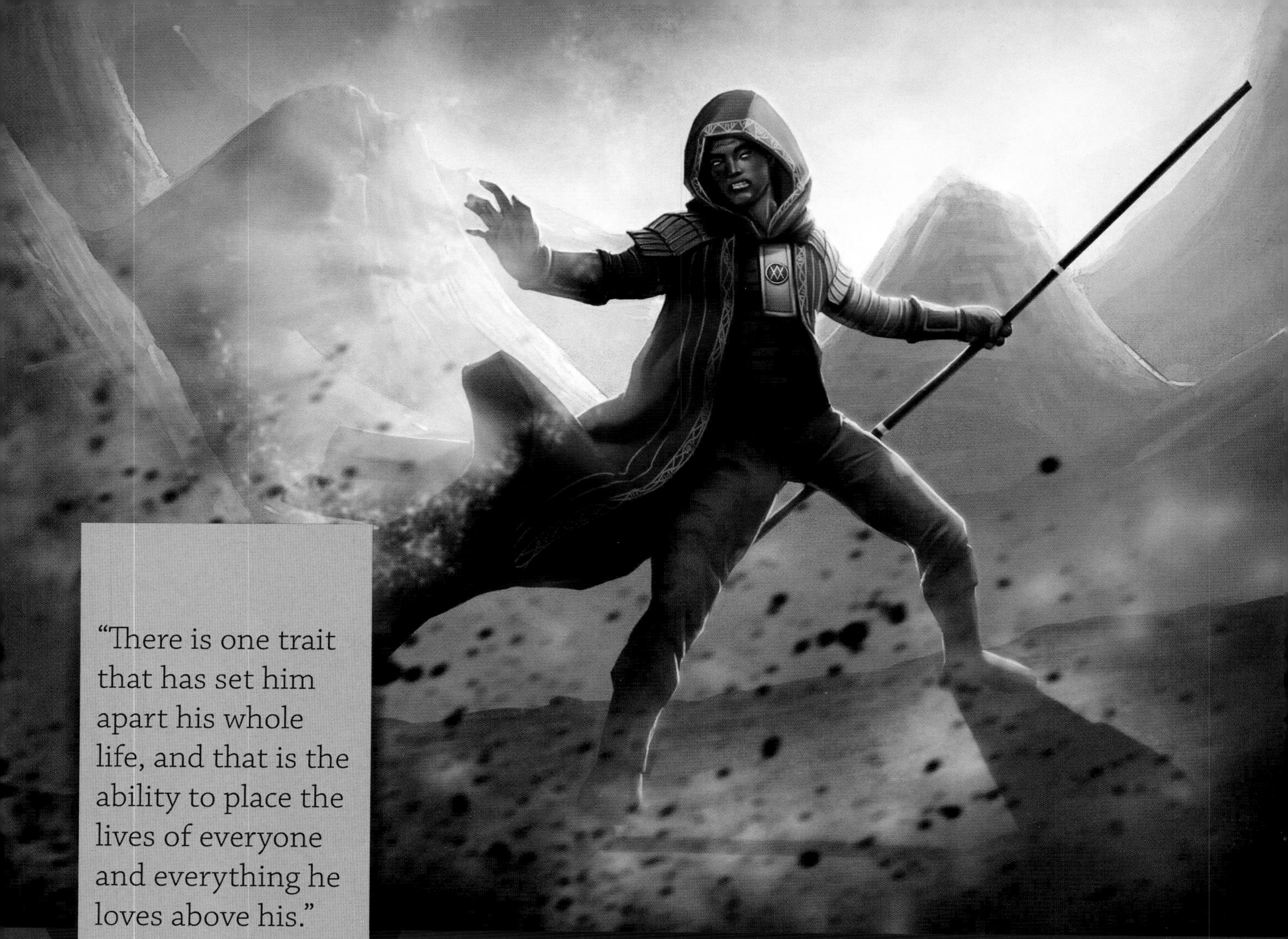

"There is one trait that has set him apart his whole life, and that is the ability to place the lives of everyone and everything he loves above his."

King Bass is, without doubt, the greatest man I have ever known. Even more so, the most peaceful, which may appear paradoxical, especially for a man who has fought in so many battles. But to illustrate my point, let us examine his choice of weapon. The reason our king carries a staff and not a sword like the rest of us is because for him, killing his enemy is a last resort.

From birth Bass was a curious and adventurous child. But there is one trait that has set him apart his whole life, and that is the ability to place the lives of everyone and everything he loves above his. In all things, all throughout his life, he has never failed in this regard. Recently, as we journeyed here to Awori, I remembered a famous story about our king. An only child, Bass and his parents owned a farm. One night, while his father was away trading produce, a fire broke out in one of the barns, trapping both livestock and one of the farm workers. Outside, Bass' mother screamed for help as the other workers and neighbors consoled her, pleading with her to leave the area. "There is nothing we can do for them now," one neighbor said to her. But as everyone fled danger, little Bass climbed to the roof of the burning barn, descending into the blaze. His mother fainted instantly. A few tense moments later, the barn doors broke open and the livestock scrambled for safety! A few more tense moments later, Bass appeared, dragging an unconscious but alive farm worker from the fire. That farm worker was my father. The next day, when asked why he ran into the burning barn so recklessly, he responded, "Because no one else would."

No other story better embodies the true character of our king. Even before he got his powers, he was a hero. And as for how he got his powers, the tale is not so different from the first. Only this time he wasn't saving my father, he was saving me.

We had planned to ambush one of General Cheng's top lieutenants. All went according to plan, but in the chaos towards the end of the attack, I was severely injured and got separated from the Ravens. I had to flee behind enemy lines. Days went by as I barely eluded Ming search parties. I was certain all I was doing was delaying my eventual capture, or worse, demise. After a while, I could go on no longer. I had gone days without food while nursing a painful injury. Just as I was about to give in, I heard footsteps. Certainly it was Ming soldiers coming to put me out of my misery. So I took a stance to defend myself. As I would have rather died than be captured by the demon Cheng. But too my surprise, it was my king. He had spent weeks alone tracking me behind enemy lines. As happy I as I was to see him, my body gave out moments later. I blacked out.

After I came to, I realized that my king had carried me for who knows how long while I was unconscious. We were just about to cross back into friendly territory, but a small battalion of Ming troops flanked us. Cornered and seeing that we had no choice, I drew my blade, apologized to Bass for drawing him into enemy territory and prepared for death. My king on the other hand simply smiled and said, "Bengu, lower your blade and stay behind me." Within seconds, Bass unleashed a series of wind attacks that completely decimated the enemy. And then in my mind it clicked. My king had accessed the power of **Yao**. My king had found the **Wind Stone**. As to how exactly he found it, well, that is a story for another tome.

"When asked why he ran into the burning barn so recklessly, he responded, 'Because no one else would'."

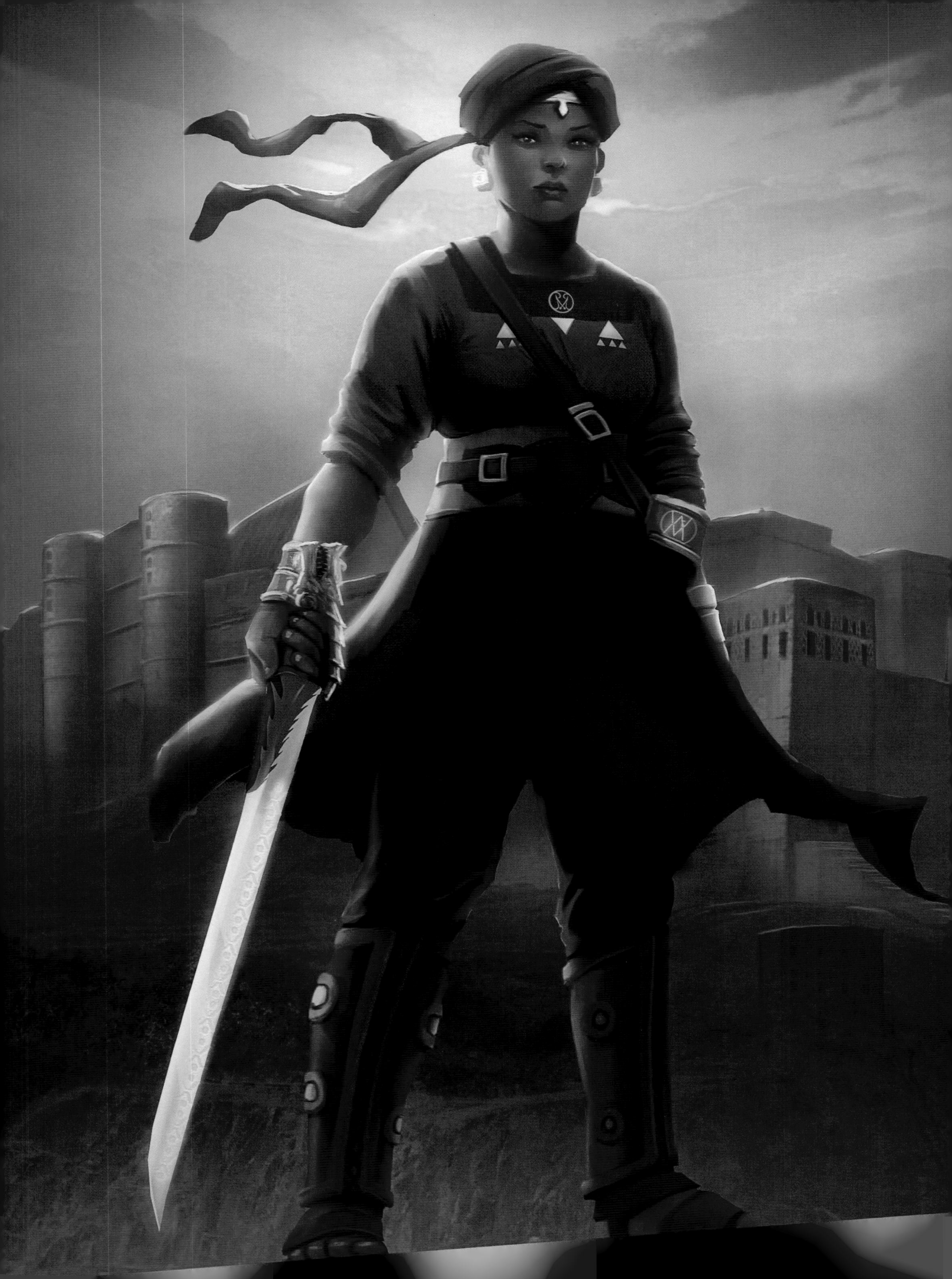

"Unity does not mean we must or should agree on all things. Unity means even in our disagreements, we respect each other enough to seek peaceful harmony in our differences"

Malika Bakwa Queen of Azzaz

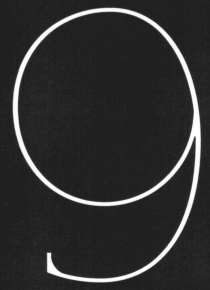

9

THE AZZAZIANS

Our Azzazian Allies

In the hour of our must desperate need, the Azzazians came like a tempest. Violently ripping through the Ming flanks on their horses, striking fear into the eyes of the enemy. This is the might of the Azzazian cavalry. Lead by their queen **Malika**, or as they call her, **The Great Unifier**, the Azzazian cavalry is one of the most deadly military units ever. The very mention of the name "Azzazian Cavalry" was enough to strike fear in the heart of the greatest of enemies. Famous for their "charge and retreat" tactic, which fooled enemies by attacking and then luring them out of formation and strategic positioning, the Azzazian Cavalry have been the subject of many heroic folklores. I once heard that the cavalry tipped the scales of a battle in which the Azzazian army was outnumbered three to one.

At the rebuke of her council, Malika and her cavalry came to our aid at the Battle of Ajaka. Their faces were concealed to make them look like Red Raven reinforcements. Their arrival gave us the much-needed advantage and we won the battle. But Cheng, being the snake that he is and always will be until we cut off his head, escaped again. This time to the far east, towards the **Kongolese Empire**.

Queen Malika coming to our aid this way was very perilous. If they were discovered, Ming could turn its sights on her Azzazian Empire. But this is the sort of inspiration queen Malika is. She would risk everything to protect not only her people, but her allies as well. Being a great leader may not even be her most important gift. For Queen Malika is an exceptional fighter. Some have even gone as far as to say that she is the best duelist to ever walk the earth. After witnessing her fight first hand, I can see why they think so. As for my thoughts on this claim, I am not sure I am ready to give her that title as of yet. However, it fills me with great joy that she is not my enemy.

Conclusion

And thus concludes the history of the great kingdom of Atala. And if history has taught me anything, I know that our future will contain even greater stories and perhaps more legends. But for now, I must resume the reality of the present. Cheng is still out there and our king has charged me with positioning the Ravens at the City of Confluence in Azzaz. "Do not argue, Bengu," he said, refusing to provide me with the full details as to why he wants us there. I suspect this has to do with Cheng. So we will be ready.

I hope this tome has provided a much-needed wealth of knowledge into our roots as Atalians. As a reader, wherever and whenever you are, I hope you find time to connect with your own roots as well. Because at the end of it all, how can we truly know who we are if we cannot identify with where we are from. That very challenge is the whole purpose of this tome.

The YouNeek YouNiverse

Coming off the hit graphic novel: E.X.O. The Legend of Wale Williams (Parts One & Two), whi[ch] was featured on CNN, Forbes, The New York Times, The Washington Post and more, **WindMake[r]: The History of Atala** is the first art book in the continuity of a shared universe of graph[ic] novels called the "YouNeek Youniverse." Dubbed "The MCU of graphic novels," the YouNe[ek] YouNiverse is a combination of individual graphic novel series (E.X.O., Malika, WindMaker et[c.) tied together with one continuous, overall plot that weaves through each individual story.

"We want to make it easy for anyone to get into comic book stories, which at the end of the d[ay] are just, well... 'Stories.' One of the inspirations behind the YouNiverse comes from somethi[ng] I see Marvel Studios doing very successfully with their movies. Marvel has masterfully crafte[d a] system of connected movies (collectively called the Marvel Cinematic Universe or "MCU") th[at] has attracted millions of casual, everyday fans that have never read a single comic book!"

Roye Okupe, Co-Founder/CEO YouNeek Studios

You can read (some titles are free to download) the rest of the titles in the shared "YouNivers[e"] at **www.youneekstudios.com**